In a proper review of the Snowy Rowles case, it is impossible to disregard my work as a novelist; because, although I did not provide Rowles with a motive, and was in no way an accessory before or after the fact, the Crown alleged that I did provide him with a method of destroying the bodies of his victims.

Three murders, three perfect murders... near the rabbit-proof fence in desolate Western Australia. Perfect - except the process was exactly as described in Arthur Upfield's crime novel *The Sands of Windee* (1931).

It had all began in 1929, when Upfield was working on the fence and plotting a new novel featuring the Aboriginal detective, Napoleon Bonaparte. His friend George Ritchie had devised a brilliant method of disposing a body in the outback, so brilliant that Upfield offered Ritchie a pound if he could come up with a flaw in the process. On October 5 1929, Upfield, Ritchie and Snowy Rowles, the northern boundary rider for the fence, all met at the Camel Station and discussed the murder method in the forthcoming book...

This is Upfield's own account of the Snowy Rowles murder case, augmented by police photographs.

www.arthurupfield.com

Arthur Upfield, 1929.

THE
MURCHISON
MURDERS

ARTHUR W. UPFIELD

ETT IMPRINT

Exile Bay

ETT IMPRINT
PO Box R1906
Royal Exchange NSW 1225
Australia

Copyright © William Upfield 2015, 2021

First published 1932
Published by ETT Imprint in 2015. Reprinted in 2018
First electronic edition published by ETT Imprint in 2015

ISBN 978-1-922473-72-1
ISBN 978-1-922473-73-8

Design by Hanna Gotlieb and Tom Thompson
Cover shows the police evidence for the case against Snowy Rowles
Cover design by Tom Thompson

THE
MURCHISON
MURDERS

To give a clear picture of the country, and to clothe in words the personalities in the most sensational murder drama that ever took place in Australia, is essential to the proper appreciation of a case containing, as it does, several features believed to be unique.

In the bush proper of Western Australia three men disappeared from human ken between December 8, 1929, and May 18, 1930, and it was not until the following February that the relatives of one, making inquiries from New Zealand, first called the attention of the police to those disappearances and started investigations that occupied many months, and entailed thousands of miles of travel, and the compilation of volumes of reports and statements.

All caused through a novelist's search for a plot to be used in a murder-mystery story.

Two views of the Government Camel Station.

Government Camel Station

The Government Camel Station is 163 miles north of the wheat town of Burracoppin, and about 75 south of the gold-mining town of Paynesville.

The homestead is a four-rooms-and-kitchen stone building, situated about 100 yards west of the vermin fence, which, from the south to the northwest coast, is some 1130 miles long – undoubtedly the longest netted fence in the world. Standing at the homestead front door, one faces east, able to see the fence and the wall of mulga scrub beyond the fence track. From the back door a few scattered acacias are the only obstructions to the view. About half a mile north-westward a double-summited hill rises from a roughly circular plain, the two summits forming the rounded humps of the animal after which the place is named – Dromedary Hill.

One familiar with the locality knows that northward along the fence at the edge of the scrub timber, there is a hut and a well named Watson's Well; that southward along the fence there is nothing until Campian is reached, 138 miles distant; that by following a westward track for 10 miles one will reach The Fountain, a stockman's hut, and, after a further ten miles, the homestead of Narndee Station to which the stockman's hut belongs.

As for people and traffic, one might wait a week, two weeks, to see a human face or a dust-coated car pass along the fence track; and only rarely did a Narndee man call when on his way to that station's paddocks east of the Camel Station.

Dry, parched, heated land in summer; brilliant, bracing, beautiful in winter.

At the Camel Station lived George Ritchie. To the Camel Station once every month came two Government boundary riders: Lance Maddison from the north, Arthur Upfield from the south. From the west at irregular intervals came a station contractor named James Ryan, and a stockman named "Snowy" Rowles. These were the men destined to play important roles in a terrific drama.

Enter "Snowy" Rowles

I first met Rowles at the Narndee outcamp, The Fountain, where he was stationed. He was then twenty-five years old; a man well- proportioned, fair-haired, blue-eyed, clean-shaven, neat in dress, and, from the feminine standpoint, better-looking than the average.

Looking backward, I can find no excuse for any one on the Murchison not liking Snowy Rowles. His appearance at a bush camp at once vanquished depression. He arrived at the Camel Station one day, late in '28, on a motor-cycle, looking for a job. It happened that the owner of Narndee had bought a bunch of mules from the Government and they were being handled by a breaker in the Dromedary Hill yards, preparatory to being taken to Narndee. Rowles offered to ride his worst mules – for exercise.

There was left no doubt in the mind of any who saw him, that he rode as well as the best in the great North-west of the State. He was offered work on Narndee, which he accepted.

His horse-riding was point No. 1 in favour of this newly- arrived stranger. The second point was an equable temper; the third a most engaging disposition; the fourth a willingness to oblige. As a fifth point, he was a good bettor and a good loser. And the sixth and most important point was a ready sense of humour.

On his arrival one day at Dromedary Hill we asked him if he'd brought any meat, as we had to eat either tinned "dog" or kangaroo. No; he hadn't. Then he had better go back to his camp (10 miles) and get some.

"Righto! You scour out the fry-pan", he urged, laughing; and away he went on his motor bike in a cloud of dust.

Expecting a fore-quarter of mutton at least, we got busy with fire and fry-pan. In half an hour he was seen dodging this way and that over the plain between the house and the hill; a spurt of dust as big as a cloud in front of his machine.

"What the devil is he doing?" demanded my companion.

John Thomas Smith, better known as "Snowy" Rowles.

"I always did think that what one wants in these parts is a pair of binoculars", I rejoined. "He'll break his neck among those rabbit burrows and rocks."

It was country over which I would not gallop a horse.

Instead of bringing back a fore-quarter of mutton Snowy Rowles mustered into the back yard a "boomer" kangaroo that he had rounded up; tailing it home like a sheep being brought in by a man on horseback.

Plots – and a Plot

In a proper review of the Snowy Rowles case, it is impossible to disregard my work as a novelist; because, although I did not provide Rowles with a motive, and was in no way an accessory before or after the fact, the Crown alleged that I did provide him with a method of destroying the bodies of his victims.

It is the ambition of many novelists who are free from the obsession of sex, to discover an original plot, or at least an original variation of an old one. Fiction plots are like nuggets of gold dug out of a unique mine. A hundred years ago this mine contained much gold; to-day nuggets are scarce, and much digging is necessary to unearth them.

Notable nuggets were discovered by: Anthony Hope in *The Prisoner of Zenda*; Burroughs in his *Tarzan of the Apes*; Rudd in his *On Our Selection*. They were golden nuggets literally as well as iguratively.

During a several weeks' stay at the Camel Station in the early winter of 1929, I thought much of the type of story to follow a psychological study – then nearing completion – of a lonely man on a desolate beach. Day by day Ritchie and I followed a simple work routine. In the morning one of us brought in the two camels on which we were working, and these were harnessed to a heavy buckboard and taught to pull it, to walk, to trot, to stop quietly at gates, and, above all, to stand still.

To us the constant driving quickly became automatic, and when labour becomes automatic one's mind is free to rove. One bitterly cold day, whilst we drove round and round Dromedary Hill, I recalled that Wilkie Collins dug up the murder-mystery nugget from the mine of golden plots. Nuggets of variation have been unearthed by such masters as Edgar Allen Poe and Sir Arthur Conan Doyle; but it appeared to me that these and lesser diggers in that field were bound by a single cast-iron set of rules. The body of a murdered person is found – formerly on the library floor; latterly on the top of a bus, beneath a lift, or other unlikely place – and then the detective has a look at the corpse, and his investigation leads inevitably to the arrest of the murderer.

Questions demanded an answer. Why a corpse? Why be satisfied with what satisfied our grandfathers? Why continue littering the pages of a novel with blood? Here, then, was a new nugget, a beautiful theme nugget, waiting to be discovered. Instead of having the same old corpse in the first chapter, as the Masters and their sheep-like followers always did, why not date a fictional murder two months before the story opens? Why not write a murder-mystery without a corpse at all? In short, why not completely destroy the body of a victim of homicide, and then permit my fictional Detective-Inspector Napoleon Bonaparte to prove, first, that a murder had been committed, secondly, how it had been committed, and, thirdly, who committed it? I could make him begin his investigation two months after the corpse had been destroyed without trace.

Difficulties

The idea was attractive, but clothing the idea with life quickly presented difficulties.

How many murderers in real life – including doctors and other intelligent persons – have failed to dispose of the bodies of their victims, despite all their ingenuity! Crippen, Landru, and Mahon come easily to mind; and Deeming's fate was inevitable. Each of them cut up their victims, and then were unable to destroy the parts. Of all killers, perhaps the Paris Bluebeard came nearest to success.

I was faced with what I may term Problem Number One. With appliances that the average person could obtain, how could a human body be so utterly destroyed that no trace of its existence should remain to damn a murderer? A crematorium, or a bath of corrosive acid, are not within the reach of ordinary people desirous of cheating justice. Putting a body down a well, even dropping it down an abandoned mine shaft and exploding tons of earth on it, would not destroy it. Although concealed, it would still exist, still menace the security of the murderer.

The Nugget is Suggested

I had decided upon the locality of the story to be written. I had gathered around me the cast of characters, had even planned a rough chart of the action; but I could not start the story because I was unable to invent a simple and effective method of destroying my intended corpse.

Whilst playing poker one night, with a cold south wind rumbling round the chimney above the roaring wood fire, I said to Ritchie:

"Can you tell me of a good way of getting rid of a man, assuming I killed him on paper? I want a method of completely destroying a human body, so that there will be no slightest trace left for Bony to find."

"What! Are you going to start another book?"

"Yes, I am. I want to write another Bony yarn, in which he gets a job of work worthy of his brains and his bush craft. I want to give him the case of his life, if I can nut out a simple way of getting rid of the eternal hackneyed corpse."

"Well, all right. Suppose I wanted to do you in. I'd kid you into the bush, and when your back was turned I'd shoot you stone dead. Then I'd gather wood and lay you on it, clothes, boots and all, pile wood over you, and burn you. In a couple of days I'd come back with a sieve, and I'd go through all the ashes with the sieve, and get out every metal object, and every piece of bone that wasn't burned up by the fire. The metal objects could be thrown down a well, and the bones I'd dolly-pot to dust. So that no chance passer would wonder what the fire really was for, I'd shoot a couple of kangaroos and burn 'em over the same place."

I went outside and looked up at the chilly stars. The very kernel of my Problem Number One was a dolly-pot to deal with the bones that an ordinary fire would not destroy. Why had I not thought of a dolly-pot? It is a common object on the Murchison, as in other parts of Australia.

Arthur Upfield with his camels, 1929.
A dolly-pot.

Anyone could possess a dolly-pot. There was one in the blacksmith's shop at the Dromedary Hill homestead.

Problem Number Two

The plot of the new novel was rushing into shape. My murderer should destroy the body of his victim in the way given; and then Bony should get to 'work, and prove − ! But what could he prove? What could he prove if there was not a particle of the body remaining for him to exhibit before a judge and jury, who require the production of a body, or identifiable parts of a body, before they will listen to a charge of murder. If my murderer carried out Ritchie's astoundingly simple method, how could my detective build up his case, though he possess superhuman intelligence? Obviously, my murderer must make one mistake in his perfect murder, because unless he did so no detective in real life, or even in fiction, could prove murder against him.

Appreciating the fact that Ritchie had supplied me with a gold nugget, I offered him a pound if he could find a flaw in it. I believe he thought that pound was going to be easy money.

The problem was compressed into a simple question. If a man did such and such and such, how could he make a fatal error? Thresh at it, argue how we would, we could not discover a flaw. It became a tantalising but intriguing conundrum: I could not solve it, nor could my friends on the Fence, at Burracoppin and at Perth.

His mind on the pound, riding a fresh horse, hatless and unshaved, and carrying a .22 bore rifle, Ritchie one day met Snowy Rowles coming to the Camel Station on his motor-cycle. Without preamble of any kind, Ritchie said:

"Hey, Snow! If I was to shoot you stone dead, drag your body over to that dead scrub, burn it thoroughly, then come hack tomorrow with a sieve and go through the ashes for the bones and the metal objects on your clothes, dump the metal objects down a well, and dolly your bones to dust, how could my crime be discovered?"

Rowles subsequently admitted that he thought Ritchie had gone mad. Muttering something about being in a hurry, he skidded away on a roaring machine, expecting at any second to feel the bite of a bullet in his back.

Ritchie remained on his horse, looking after him in astonishment. Not until several hours later did he realise that the joke was against himself.

The Solution

The weeks passed.

I went back to my fence section; using two camels drawing a heavy hooded cart tandem fashion. 163 miles was that section; and at the completion of the first trip I had not worked out the solution of my problem, and I had practically given up the idea of ever finding that beautiful fiction nugget. Ritchie failed to earn the pound; Maddison was no help; Rowles did not succeed.

Then one morning, when most certainly I was not thinking about murder problems, but was gazing down my shaft camel's gaping throat whilst I struggled to put on him a pair of winkers, the solution flashed through my mind like the stab of a searchlight. My murderer could carry out Ritchie's method in every detail and yet leave a clue for Bony to find, follow up, and convict him. Where he could make, his fatal slip was in his lack of knowledge of his victim's war record. Within three seconds, whilst I gazed stupidly at Curley, the camel, I saw placed in position the last piece of a jigsaw puzzle.

The plot of the new novel was complete to its last detail. Further weeks passed in another trip to Burracoppin and back.

Then the Inspector reversed the positions held by Ritchie and myself, and from the interior of a boundary rider's cart I transferred my writing to the comfortable stone-built house, where night after night I wrote, aided by the blessed peacefulness of the bush.

October 5, 1929, was a Sunday. According to my diary for that evening there were present in the Camel Station homestead "drawing-room" Ritchie, Rowles, the Inspector's son, the north boundary-rider, and myself.

Arthur Upfield's dray, containing his writing desk.

Those others remember that night particularly, for a reason I do not propose to state; I remember it particularly because it was the last opportunity I had to discuss my Problem Number Two, which was to locate a weak spot in Problem Number One. It was not then discussed with intense interest, because every one at this time was fully conversant with these two problems, but it was an incidence which was used by the Crown to establish through several witnesses that Snowy Rowles was conversant with the method of body destruction used in my novel *The Sands of Windee* published eighteen months later.

Ryan and Lloyd

Rowles left his employment on Narndee Station on October 30 of the same year, and took up the work of fox poisoning for a living; he being now the owner of an old but serviceable motor-car. Operating in the locality, he camped with me several nights on various dates, and if I had had no domestic ties it is likely that I should have joined him, for by this time I was becoming sick of the Vermin Fence, and wanted to have a look at the far north. Rowles was always welcome. He was an excellent guest, willing to do his share of the chores, and anxious to put in his share of the rations when his stay was extended.

About November 24 a contractor named James Ryan arrived at my homestead on his way to Burracoppin. About forty years old, he was what he looked, a naval man. He drove his own newly- purchased Dodge runabout car, and on his departure he promised to bring back for me rations and mail, neither of which I had received for some five or six weeks.

About the first day of December Rowles arrived from the direction of Youanmi. He wanted to know if Ryan had returned, and told me that he hoped, when Ryan did return, to join him on a trip to the far north-west. I did not know that Ryan intended pulling out from Narndee and was not interested, since neither Rowles nor Ryan was working for the Department; therefore they did not concern me, particularly as I had heard that the owner of Narndee was slackening hands.

Challi Bore showing Ryan's camp on Narndee Station. Constable Hearn and an Aboriginal tracker sieving ashes at Challi Bore searching for the remains of Ryan and Lloyd.

Rowles appeared anxious for Ryan's return, and left me to run south to meet him. He did so at the 96-mile rainshed, and as his car had broken down, he returned with Ryan, who had brought with him as a mate a young athletic man named George Lloyd.

The party stayed with me that night, but it did not seem certain that Rowles would accompany Ryan and Lloyd to the former's camp until the next morning. During the evening Ryan sang songs in a really fine voice, accompanied by Lloyd on a brand new accordion.

Early the next morning the three departed, and either that afternoon or the next Rowles and Lloyd passed through the Camel Station on their way to the 100-peg where Rowles's old car had broken down. They brought the car back, and left it in a shed.

That was the last I saw of either Lloyd or Ryan.

The Inspector arrived from Burracoppin on December 10; Ritchie on the day previous. The day after the Inspector left for the north, Ritchie went up the Fence to Watson's Well, where a prospector named James Yates was camped. On his return he brought the information that Rowles, Ryan and Lloyd, instead of coming past the Camel Station homestead to reach the north track, had travelled along the north boundary of the hill paddock, round the back of the hill, and had passed through the rabbit fence at Watson's Well to get to that north track.

There was nothing significant about this. Ritchie did not make it clear to me – I was not that interested, anyway – that Yates had seen only Rowles, who told him that Ryan and Lloyd were walking through the scrub looking for timber with which to build a sheep-yard. To me, it appeared as Rowles had said. Ryan had pulled out from a bad contract, and he was with him on the long trip to the north-west. He had laid his plans rather well.

Christmas 1929

Late in the afternoon of Christmas Eve the north boundary-rider and I left for Youanmi to buy a sucking pig and a bottle of beer, and there on the steps of the Youanmi Hotel stood Snowy Rowles.

George Ritchie at work.
Narndee Station, as it is now.

"Hello? What are you doing here?" I asked. "Thought you were in the north-west with Ryan and Lloyd."

"Oh! We got as far as Mount Magnet," Rowles replied. "Ryan stays put, so I borrowed his truck to come over here for Christmas."

It came out later that he told my companion he had bought the truck from Ryan for £80.

Now there was nothing extraordinary in this story. Long before then Rowles had told us that his grandfather had come to his rescue with money on a former occasion, and that he was thinking of applying for a loan with which to purchase a good second-hand truck. And, too, Ryan was one of those unfortunate men who are fascinated by hotels, and who sometimes will attempt to sell their shirts, let alone a runabout truck, to buy a few more drinks. It was easy to picture Ryan, semi-intoxicated, generously granting Rowles permission to take his truck, with Lloyd, who did not drink, in the offing earnestly waiting to get his mate out of town.

Not the slightest suspicion that anything was wrong entered our minds. No one of the three was a close friend of ours.

Shocks

Meanwhile the depression had fallen like a blight, the staff had been reduced, and my section of fence had been altered to run 100 miles north, and 100 miles south of Burracoppin.

It was at the 78-mile peg south of the Department's headquarters' town that the Inspector came along, to say:

"You remember Jack Lemon, who works on Narndee"

I did. Lemon had taken Snowy Rowles's place. I remembered Lemon telling me a few months before how he had come from the East and had "palled up" with a man on the boat; how they had tramped to the Murchison from Perth; and how his pal had got a job on Wydgee Station, and himself one on Narndee; these two stations adjoining.

The Inspector went on to explain to me that Carron, Lemon's friend, resigned his employment or was paid off, and had left Wydgee Station in

Snowy Rowles with Ryan's ute, photograph by Arthur Upfield 1929.
Arthur Upfield resetting a section of the Rabbit-Proof fence 1928.

company with Rowles, some time in May, 1930. It was also known that Rowles had cashed Carron's pay cheque, and had bought beer out of the money at Paynesville, a mining town east of Mount Magnet. It appeared that Lemon had sent a reply-paid telegram to Rowles at Youanmi asking for information regarding his friend, and Rowles had not replied either by telegram or letter.

"It is likely that Louis Carron's disappearance would never have been remarked had he not been a confirmed letter-writer. Up to the time he left Wydgee Station he had written regularly to friends in New Zealand and to his pal, John Lemon, at Narndee.

All this the Inspector learned during his trip north – his section extended to the 421-mile peg – in February, 1931, ten months after Carron and Rowles had driven away from The Fountain in Ryan's truck. Jack Lemon was the last man to see Carron, who promised to write and tell him how he got on in his search for a new job.

My untrained imagination jumped at a solution of this little mystery. Carron, paid off with a cheque, goes with Snowy, and they decide to purchase a case of beer and have a peaceful or private carousal in the bush – much cheaper than drinking at an hotel. Naturally, in possession of a case of beer, they both become stung. A quarrel arises, there is a fight, and Carron gets killed.

"That might be how it happened," the Inspector agreed. "Anyway, the detectives are scouring the whole country in a search for Carron's body. It looks pretty black against Snowy."

"Have they arrested him?"

"No, not yet. He's working now on a station called Hill View, a couple of hundred miles or so north of Youanmi."

"Then it mightn't be Snowy," I objected.

"But they know that Carron left the Fountain with Rowles. They know that Rowles cashed Carron's cheque at the Paynesville hotel. And they know that Rowles never answered Lemon's telegram."

Three weeks after this conversation the Inspector returned again from a north trip. He said grimly:

"Ryan and Lloyd are missing now. They haven't been seen since they left the Camel Station in December, 1929."

I must have looked a half-wit, standing with my mouth open in utter astonishment. And whilst thus standing came the next shock. "And they've found Carron's charred remains near the one-eight-three mile hut – a ring, false teeth, a dental plate, bones. "Go on?" I urged desperately.

"And when they went to arrest Snowy Rowles they recognised him as a man who escaped from the Dalwallinu lock-up after having been convicted for burglary in 1928. They haven't arrested him for murder but for gaol escape, so that the detectives will have whips of time to complete their investigations into the disappearances of Carron, Ryan and Lloyd."

It was all so incredible that for several minutes my mind refused to accept it. I found it harder to believe that Rowles was a burglar than a suspected murderer. No man was less like even my modern conception of a burglar. He had never stolen anything from me, or so little as a piece of hoop-iron from the Government Station. He might have killed Carron during a drunken brawl; but. . . a common burglar!

"Looks like he put that book lot of yours into practice," said a man with the Inspector.

"Seems that you and Ritchie were the last people to see Ryan and Lloyd alive in the company of Snowy Rowles," added the Inspector. "If you take my advice you'll write out a statement to the police. They know all about you, and all about your hunt for a murder-plot."

Bush Psychology

There are many points in this case which are sure to perplex a reader unfamiliar with the psychology and habits of the bushman. During the trial several witnesses were obliged to interrupt their evidence to explain why something was done, or how something else came about. When preparing his case, Mr. Gibson, the Crown Prosecutor, had the assistance

Camp at the 183 mile peg of the rabbit-proof fence.

of Detective-Sergeant Harry Manning, who conducted the police investigation – assistance of great value, because Manning is an experienced bushman. On the other side, Mr. Curran, defending Rowles, seemed not to have the same assistance, even from Rowles, who was a superb bushman.

Here is one illustration: At the inquest Mr. Curran said to witness Lance Maddison:

"There are hundreds of square miles of dense scrub around the hut (the hut near the bore about where the remains of Carron were found); don't you think it would be foolish for a man to try to burn evidence of a crime around the hut?"

"I can't say," replied the cautious witness.

To a city dweller, Mr. Curran's question would have appeared quite logical. In point of fact, that hut was an ideal locality, as will be explained a little later. To the city-dweller, also, the most astonishing feature of the disappearance of the three men is that no one missed them, or thought to inquire for them, until nearly twelve months had elapsed. Yet to the bushman there is nothing singular about that, mainly because a large part of the population of Central Australia is a floating population, to which all three missing men belonged.

The Hounds of the Law

In early January, 1931, John Lemon interviewed Constable Hearn, of Mount Magnet, and reported the fact that his friend, Louis Carron, had not written to him since he had left his camp on Narndee Station – that formerly occupied by Snowy Rowles, named The Fountain. At this time Hearn had already received a letter from a Mr. Jackson, of Dunedin, N.Z., making inquiries for Carron. But not until February 17 did he, accompanied by a veteran bushman, Constable McArthur, set out from Mount Magnet to make inquiries.

Because John Lemon understood from his friend and Rowles on their departure from his camp that they were going to Wiluna in search of employment, Constables Hearn and McArthur started their inquiries from that town – 200 north of west. Drawing a blank at Wiluna, they came back to the Vermin Fence and then south to the Camel Station, which they made their headquarters; approximately another 200 miles.

Such is the peculiar nature of the soil on the Murchison that tracks made by carts and waggons remain visible for years. Up and down the Fence, and off every cross road, there are in evidence to-day seldom used tracks originally made by the waggon carting the Fence posts, and drays bringing out of the bush their loads of sandalwood. And over all those tracks might be driven a car.

On this huge area of country, to find the remains of a man which might have been burned or buried ten months before, seemed to be closely allied to the problem of finding the needle in the haystack. And yet in a remarkably short space of time the hounds of the law found evidences of a large fire in the vicinity of a bore at the 183-mile peg – twenty miles north from the Camel Station, on the No. 1 Vermin Fence.

At this point the Fence track passes through dense narrow-leafed mulga. Here there is a little-used gate; and should the curious pass through this gate and follow the little-used track for half a mile he would arrive at a small iron hut set amidst the dense scrub, which hides it entirely from the traveller on the Fence track. There was no water at this place, and the section rider, Lance Maddison, had occasion to go there only about twice a year to report on the condition of the hut. 300 yards farther west, the police came to a bore, quite out of order and, therefore, useless; and in the vicinity of this bore they found the site of a large fire. Slight trails of ashes led them still deeper into the bush, where they discovered two more heaps of ashes. Examination of these showed that the heaps had been made with ashes carried from the main fire, for beneath the heaps the grass was unburned, proving that the ashes had been dumped there when cold.

Among the ashes they found what were thought to be pieces of skull-bone, human bones, animal bones, charred woollen material, and a bone button. They found, too, among the ashes of the smaller heaps, artificial teeth, gold clips from a dental plate, metal eyelets from boots or shoes, a wedding ring, several strange wire stitches, etc.

Arrow pointing to the area where ashes, ring and dental plate were found in the Murchison bones case

These exhibits, with their report, were forwarded to police headquarters. It was thereupon decided to send Detective- Sergeant Manning north to take charge of the case.

Murder in Fact and Fiction

The fictional murder case that engaged the attention of Inspector Bonaparte in The Sands of Windee was paralleled to an extraordinary extent by the actual murder case investigated by Detective-Sergeant Manning. Manning's task was both greater and less than that presented to Bonaparte; and, the following points of similarity seem worthy of note, as indicating why the Crown suggested that Rowles adopted the book method of body destruction in part, in the case of Louis Carron.

MANNING

Police examined ashes of a large fire 10 months after Carron disappeared.

Police found in ashes human bones, false teeth, dental plate fasteners, a wedding ring, etc

Police found in ashes a piece of melted lead of equal weight to an 0.32 bore bullet.

Police found in ashes, besides human hones, plenty of animal bones.

Police found an iron camp-oven which, it was assumed, was used to smash up the bones of Carron.

Manning investigated a careless attempt to destroy a human body.

BONAPARTE

Bony examined ashes of a large fire two months after Marks was reported missing.

Bony found in ashes one boot-sprig. Also a silver disc in the fork of a tree some distance from the scene of the murder.

Bony found in ashes three pieces of melted lead, each of equal weight to an 0.44 bore bullet.

Bony found in ashes no human bones, but plenty of animal bones.

Bony found that a prospector's iron dolly-pot had been used to pound to dust the bones of Marks.

Bony investigated the almost perfect murder, the body of Marks having been most efficiently destroyed.

Detective-Sergeant Manning.
Upfield's own drawing of Bony.

Manning found in one ash heap bones which he took for human finger hones.	Bony found in the ashes bones which he sent to his headquarters to determine if they were human finger bones or kangaroo paw bones.

Manning found in one ash heap bones which he took for human finger hones.

Manning had to convince a real life judge and jury that Carron had been murdered by Rowles.

Manning is par excellence a bushman.

Bony found in the ashes bones which he sent to his headquarters to determine if they were human finger bones or kangaroo paw bones.

Bony was diverted from bringing his case to a judge and jury because logically he would have failed to convince them.

Bony, having the tracking powers of his aboriginal mother and the reason-powers of his white father, was a super- bushman.

Step by Step

On leaving Perth Sergeant Manning proceeded to Mount Magnet, where he conferred with Constables McArthur and Hearn. It happened that when Mr. Jackson's letter was received Constable Hearn was due for annual leave, but he requested that his leave might be postponed that he might ascertain Carron's fate. Constable McArthur was sent to relieve him; and, therefore, when Manning set out for the scene of the assumed murder, he was accompanied by Constable Hearn.

A second and more careful examination, made with a sieve, brought lo light a burned human molar tooth having a cavity on the biting surface which might have been filled by an amalgam. The camp-oven was found near the main fire, and Manning saw that ash still adhered to the outside. It seemed probable that it had been used to transport some of the ashes and bones to those other heaps, because the grass beneath the smaller heaps had been dumped in those several places when cold, as I have already stated.

Manning measured the area of the main fire-site and found it to be eight feet by six. Evidence of the heat was provided by a coffee-tin that lay on the ground several feet from the ashes. The side of the tin facing

Arrow pointing to where charred remains were found in the Murchison bones case.

the fire was badly burned. He ascertained from tracks made by a set of motor or truck tyres that a vehicle had been driven from the direction of the fence gate, and, after passing near the site of the fire, had turned and gone back.

Routine Work

Began then for Sergeant Manning that part of a detective's work which is seldom made much of in crime fiction – the taking of statements. Obviously, the first man to approach was John Lemon, Carron's friend. Already Manning had a description of Carron, supplied by Mr. Jackson. Carron was about 27 years of age, of medium build and erect carriage, with a sandy complexion, and an abrupt manner of speaking. Manning wanted to know from Lemon if Carron had false teeth; to which Lemon said: "Yes"; since he had often seen his friend cleaning them. He did not know where those teeth had been made, or by whom. And thus a line of inquiry started out from Western Australia to Hamilton, New Zealand, which resulted in a dentist named Sims being found who had made Carron a complete lower denture, consisting of diatoric teeth, and an upper partial denture being fixed to Carron's sound teeth by two gold clips.

And thirteen diatoric teeth, four pin teeth, and two gold clips had been found in the various ash heaps.

"Did Carron wear a wedding ring?"

"Yes," replied Lemon. "He wore a ring so tightly fitting that he once said he would have to have it filed off."

A second line of inquiry began, this time towards Carron's wife, Mrs. Brown, in New Zealand. (It should be explained that "Carron" had assumed this name in order to overcome the objection of his wife to his leaving New Zealand.) She remembered the ring, remembered when it was bought and at which shop in Auckland, N.Z. Eventually, Mr. A. T. Long examined the ring. He had sold it to Mrs. Brown in December, 1925. He knew the ring because of its markings, it N.Z. patents number;

and he also knew that a workman in his shop had altered the size in an inexperienced manner.

From John Lemon, Sergeant Manning worked back toward Wydgee Station, via Wheelock, a prospector, Worth, a bookkeeper, and Beasley, the manager. The date on which Mr. Worth made out and Mr. Beasley signed Carron's pay cheque for 25/0/07 was ascertained. On Wydgee it was further learned that Carron had sent to a Perth jeweller's two watches for repair, and these watches had been returned, each in a separate box. Yes, the boxes contained wire stitches similar to those found in the ashes.

Out went another line of inquiry. The jewellers said that a Mr. Stone, a box manufacturer, made the boxes for them. And Mr. Stone recognised the wire stitches as those made by one of his machines which had a slight defect causing the defect in the stitches found among the ashes. Back again to the jewellers, who stated that the same watches they had repaired for Carron had been sent them for further repairs from Messrs. Fleming & Co., at Mount Magnet. A Mr. Male, of Fleming & Co., recalled having sent the watches to the Perth jewellers, and described the man who brought them to him – a man he knew as "Snowy" Rowles.

Lemon had said that his friend and Rowles left him for Wiluna in search of work. Constable Hearn could not hear anything of either man when he made inquiries in Wiluna. Manning now followed the trail. He camped at the Camel Station homestead, he travelled north along the fence to the gate at the 206-mile, and eastward then for eighteen miles to Youanmi. And at Youanmi he found that Rowles was well known.

The detective went through the books of Mr. Jones, the licensee of the. Youanmi Hotel, tracing various cheques cashed, and dates on which Rowles had booked in. Then to Paynesville, miles westward, to gain information about a cheque made out by Mr. Edward Moses, when he learned of the transaction regarding the tender of tender of Carron's Wydgee cheque for £25/0/7. And then back again to Narndee Station, where further information was obtained from the station books.

Hundreds of miles were traversed in a motor car, filling books with place-names, distances, dates, and names of persons. Eventually the detective had the name of every man working in the district at the time

Snowy Rowles hut.

Carron disappeared. Precisely as did Bony in Windee, he made out his list of "fish," among which might be the "sting- ray." He had gathered that a man named Upfield, who wrote novels, was in charge of the Camel Station a few months prior to the disappearance of Carron. He learned from a man named Ritchie of Upfield's search for an effective method of corpse destruction. He knew that the man last seen with Carron was called "Snowy" Rowles, who since then had become employed on Hill View Station; and that Rowles had an excellent character, was a fine bushman, and owned his own runabout truck.

Yes, he had bought the truck from a man named Ryan. Where was Ryan? Oh! He had left the district with a man named Lloyd. He had taken with him a valuable compass and other things belonging to Narndee Station.

Strange!

And now information began to pour in regarding Ryan and Lloyd. Circumstances in connection with them had taken on a sinister light in view of the discovery of Carron's remains.

The detective's interest in Ryan and Lloyd was fully aroused. Where was Ryan? Last heard of at Mount Magnet, and, on Manning's reaching Mount Magnet, he found that nothing was known of Ryan, or of Lloyd, his mate: and certainly they had not stayed there during the Christmas of 1929.

Returning to Narndee later, Manning, with Constable Hearn, Mr. Bogle, part-owner and manager of Narndee, and Douglas Bell, a half-caste who had worked for Ryan before Ryan left for Burracoppin, motored down to Challi Bore, Ryan's camp, and there discovered eight sites of fires similar to that at the 183-mile Rabbit Department Reserve, among the ashes of which were found eyelets of boots or shoes, metal parts of an accordion (Lloyd had owned one), and a quantity of bones burned and broken up so small as to defy any expert to say if they were human or animal remains.

Now there were three men of whom nothing could be learned after they had been last seen in the company of this "Snowy" Rowles. To Manning, as to any other reasoning man, it now appeared that among the facts he had gleaned were those that strongly supported the assumption that Rowles was a murderer thrice over. Motive was evident – the motive of gain. Rowles owned a truck possessed formerly by one of two mates, and he had cashed a cheque made out for wages paid to a third man. Certain relics had been found at the 183-mile Rabbit Department Reserve among the ashes of a big fire, and at Challi Bore eight big fires had consumed at the least boots and or shoes and an accordion.

It admits of little doubt that sergeant Manning and the two constables were convinced that Louis Carron's body had been destroyed at the 183-mile Government Reserve and that Ryan and Lloyd had been similarly destroyed at Challi Bore. Being bushmen they arrived at certain facts:

Three men had disappeared.

Each of the three when last seen alive was in the company of Rowles.

At Ryan's camp near Challi Bore were the sites of eight large fires, and the very first question which arose was: What had been burned in those eight fires? Answer: Boots, clothing and an accordion. Assuming that Ryan and Lloyd decided, preparatory to leaving, to jettison worn boots and clothes, and that the accordion having in some manner been broken, it was also discarded, still, as bushmen leaving a temporary camp they most certainly would not have gone to the trouble of burning those articles. They would have dropped them to the ground, packed up the necessary gear, and left. Only one construction could be put upon the action of the man who lit those fires. He wished to destroy something of vital import, something that would prove that Ryan and Lloyd no longer lived, no longer required boots and clothes and an accordion.

(This contrary to Mr. Curran's remarks at the inquest that no man wishing to destroy evidence of a crime would do so in the vicinity of a hut.) The locality of the 183-mile Reserve was an ideal one for the purpose. Lance Maddison, the boundary rider, stated that he never camped there. There was no fresh water. The hut was half a mile west of the fence, and bushmen do not travel one full mile without necessity. His duty compelled him to visit the hut – but not the bore – twice every year to effect repairs. None but Maddison went there.

A Bush Detective's Conclusions

Manning's probable reasoning might be put thus:

"Assuming that a man intended to copy the details of Upfield's murder plot, and that he burned the body of his victim in the open bush, the first stockman who chanced to pass the site of the fire would examine the ashes, and would logically ask himself: 'What fool went to the trouble of burning a kangaroo here?'

"In Central Australia kangaroo-shooters would not earn tobacco money if they spent time burning the carcases of kangaroos in the open bush; but they most certainly would burn carcases of animals they shot near a dwelling or a water-dam to destroy pollution.

"Whoever burned Carron's body near the hut and bore at the 183-mile Reserve knew the plot of Upfield's book, and appreciated the value – to himself – of allaying suspicion regarding a fire site. Wherever he destroyed Carron's body, he had to create a false reason as to the purpose of the fire, besides providing a superficial reason for the situation of the fire.

"That Government Reserve is an excellent place in two respects. Those respects are applicable also to Challi Bore. Maddison at the hut, and Ryan at his camp, would assuredly burn carcases from time to time: Maddison from duly, Ryan for his own health. Maddison would burn carcases of kangaroos that had lingered at the bore – smelling the water – till they died; and Ryan would burn the carcases of kangaroos he shot during his work and took into his camp for meat; mutton from Narndee not being regularly purchased. At both places would be a quantity of animal bones, and at both places the burning of animal bones would be a normal task.

"To sum up: Whoever destroyed those three men had first to find a place where a fire would not arouse suspicion, and had then to avert suspicion of the real reason of the fires by providing evidence that kangaroo carcases had been burned for a normal reason. Both at Challi Bore and the Reserve a chance visitor would remark that at the former

Ryan had left a clean camp, and at the letter the boundary-rider had recently done his work.

"It remains to be explained, if only animal carcases were destroyed, why the burned bones should further have been broken up small."

By this, or an almost similar chain of reasoning, Sergeant Manning would be entitled to argue that the man calling himself "Snowy" Rowles either had killed the three men for their small property effect, or knew what had become of them. If Rowles had indeed killed those three, he must have planned to do so. It was highly improbable that he would be roused to three separate killings by passion or on abnormal impulse. It the first assumption was correct, Rowles must be thoroughly cold blooded and callous – a cunning and highly dangerous personality.

Rounding Up Rowles

So it came about that Sergeant Manning and Constables Hearn and Penn travelled to Hill View Station, dressed in worn bushmen's clothing. There they learned that Rowles was stationed at the outcamp several miles from the homestead: and, instead of travelling direct to the outcamp, they made a wide detour, planning to reach the outcamp from the opposite direction and at a time when Rowles would be out on his work. Had Rowles been at home he would have thought the police officers were merely kangaroo shooters, or prospectors.

But Rowles was not at his hut when the police arrived, and it was not until 2.30 on the following afternoon that he drove up in a sulky. Manning then was a little distance away in the bush; but the other two policemen were nearby their car. Rowles began to unharness his horse from the sulky, and whilst he led it away Constable Hearn took from the back of the sulky a 0.22 bore rifle. Having let the horse go, Rowles returned to the sulky, where Hearn was casually examining the rifle, and Penn and Manning converged upon him.

Manning then recognised Rowles as a man wanted for gaol- breaking, whose name was John Thomas Smith, Manning said:

"How long have you been known as Rowles?"

To which Rowles replied: "You know very well who I am, and if I had known who you were, you wouldn't have got me so easily."

Manning said that, they were looking for a man named Carron, who was last seen in his, Rowles's, company. They were also looking for James Ryan and George Lloyd.

"What are you trying to put over me now, Manning?" Rowles demanded.

To which the Detective-Sergeant counter-questioned: "Where did you get the utility truck over in the shed?"

"I bought it from Ryan," Rowels said. "I can soon satisfy you on that point."

It appears that there was a small box nailed to the door of the hut, in which the key was left; and when the door had been opened they all entered the hut, where Manning and Hearn each picked up a 0.32-bore rifle, both weapons proving to be loaded. Manning asked Rowles if everything in the hut was his property, and Rowles said it was, excepting the rifles, a sewing machine, and a gramophone.

Permission then was given the suspect to cook for himself a meal, and whilst he was doing this the police began searching the hut. A pair of hair-clippers found in a drawer of the sewing- machine (a most unusual object to be found in a stockman's hut) Rowles said he had bought from one Sher Ali for 12/6. On a high shelf was a parcel wrapped in newspaper. When one of the policemen reached for it, Rowles said:

"Where the hell did you get that? I know nothing about it."

The parcel contained a wrist-watch, three shirts, a razor marked as being made expressly for a firm in New Zealand, a watch-chain, and a pair of scissors.

Later the police went to the utility truck with Rowles, and found set in the dashboard an open-faced watch that Rowles said was there when he bought the truck from Ryan.

Without doubt these two watches furnished the most damning evidence against Rowles. Both bore marks that Manning traced to the Perth jewellers, Levinson & Sons. The marks made on each watch tallied with record cards that proved that the firm had received the watches from Louis J. Carron, Wydgee Station, on April 11, 1930, and that, as was the custom, the watches had been returned to Carron in particular boxes, held by certain wire stitches.

At a later date, it transpired, Rowles himself sent the watches to Fleming & Co., of Mount Magnet, who dispatched them to Levinson & Sons. There could be no argument, therefore, that Rowles did not know what the parcel he disowned contained.

After Rowles had eaten a meal he asked to be allowed to change his moleskin trousers and flannel into a blue serge suit. Detective-Sergeant Manning pointed out that it was hardly necessary, for he had a long dusty ride ahead; but Rowles persisted, and was allowed to change before the car journey to Meekathara was started, a distance of approximately 80 miles.

Statements and Admissions

The following morning Detective-Sergeant Manning visited Snowy Rowles in the Meekathara gaol and obtained a statement from him regarding his association with Louis J. Carron, and a second statement regarding his association with James Ryan and George Lloyd. When Rowles had signed these two long documents, he said:

"What are you going to do with the truck?" Then: "A man must have a kink to do this sort of thing. I am sorry I did not take my old lady's advice." (This sounds genuine, since Rowles always referred to his mother as "my old lady.") "She wanted me to give myself up when I escaped from Dalwallinu, and if I'd taken her advice I would have had that all over by now, and would not have had this other thing to face.

"What other thing are you referring to?" Manning asked, for Rowles had not then been charged with murder but with goal-breaking.

"Oh," replied Rowles; "the less said about that, the better." Subsequently Rowles was taken to Perth and charged with breaking and entering, and sentenced to three years' imprisonment. Had Rowles not committed burglary, the Crown doubtless would have been obliged to arraign him on a capital charge at the June Criminal Sessions, 1930, when time would not have permitted the attendance of three important New Zealand witnesses.

Where Rowles Failed

Months of hard work followed the arrest of Snowy Rowles for breaking gaol at Dalwallinu. The correspondence with the New Zealand police regarding identification of the teeth and the ring found among the ashes near a lonely bush hut was enormous. Since the witnesses, Mrs. Brown (Carron's wife), Mr. Sims, the dentist, and Mr. Long, the jeweller, could not be extradited, they could but be persuaded to travel to Western Australia in the interests of justice. Their expenses and remuneration for loss of time in their businesses cost the State £1,000.

Eminent pathologists studied the bones Sergeant Manning had brought down from the Murchison. The Government Pathologist would not say if the pieces of skull bone belonged once to the head of a white man or a blackfellow, but after further study Dr. McKenzie gave it as his opinion that the bones belonged to the skull of a while man.

And those few bones that were fitted together into larger pieces were the only human bones identifiable from the remains of three men. Had the slayer of Louis J. Carron further broken up the pieces of skull – as it can pardonably he assumed that he did in the case of the bones of Ryan and Lloyd – it could not have been proved that a human body had been destroyed at the 183- mile reserve. Had the slayer of Carron sieved the ashes for those metal objects he would have escaped the net Manning drew around him with quiet persistence; for the Crown had to prove that Carron's remains were among the ashes before it could hope to prove that Rowles had killed him.

That Rowles did not smash into smaller pieces those few portions of a human skull, that he did not sift carefully through the ashes for metal objects, can only be attributed to his belief that those three men from Central Australia's floating population would never be missed; and that, after all, the care with which he destroyed Ryan and Lloyd was not necessary with regard to Carron.

Pre-Trial Impressions

The most sensational murder trial in the history of West Australia came before Mr. Justice Draper and a jury on Thursday, March 10, and continued until late on the following Saturday week. An unusual feature of the case was that Rowles's defence was being kept a close secret, despite the efforts of keen pressmen to get a "line" on it. Public interest was enormous, and public opinion – created by the inquest – was heavily against the accused man, even in the botanical gardens surrounding the Court, where I waited my call as one of the many witnesses.

Sitting on a seat beneath an English oak from which the acorns were falling, with the cooing of a dove, the twittering of several pigeons and numerous small birds in my ears, my mind was oppressed by a sense of unreality – as though I dreamed an ill dream, yet was fully conscious I was dreaming. Sometimes that glimpse of the interior of the court, revealing to me the tense faces of the jurymen, indicated that there was being staged a theatrical drama, for which all the actors had been released, and myself one of them; that it was a play within a play; and that presently it would be over, and we all would then realise how great a play it had been.

But, the ever-present dread lurking at the back of the mind, like the knowledge that one is only dreaming, produced a kind of stunning horror that banished from the play-goer the gay mood of the play.

The sense of unreality was combined with a depressing sense of inevitability. I was like the man to whom the future has been revealed. I knew that presently I should hear my name called in a loud voice, as it were an actor summoned by a call-boy. But beyond that point I knew nothing. The actor has had experience; he knows just what he will see when he goes on the stage, and what he will say. I had had no previous experience of a court-room, nor had I the slightest idea of the questions I should be asked. Doubtless questions would be put for the purpose of trapping me, and if I wished to avoid being trapped I must remain clear-headed. Panic seized me for a little while when I found that I could not remember several dates that had been burned on my brain by constant repetition.

New impressions gained ascendancy. The power of the law became something tangible, shaping, like an octopus. Within that great stone building lived an octopus whose many tentacles had reached as far away as the Murchison, and farther still, to New Zealand.

A tentacle had come out writhing, feeling for and fastening about a young man whose gameness and sunny nature had made him ever a welcome guest. And with terrible quickness the tentacle had been withdrawn, wrapped about Snowy Rowles, who never again would laughingly chase us on his motor-cycle, and make and accept outrageous bets. And other tentacles of this great octopus called the Law came outward from Perth, dexterously searching for some fifty of us, until one by one we had been found, examined, drawn from as far away as New Zealand, to testify against Snowy Rowles.

I may state, in parenthesis, that without doubt a great majority of the Crown witnesses wanted to believe that Rowles was innocent of the charge laid against him, and would have welcomed with joy the production of proof that he was not guilty. Had it been established that he was innocent, his return to the Murchison would have been a triumphal progress.

We witnesses knew more than those city people who had carefully read our evidence given at the inquest. We had been moving behind the scenes, as it were. We were conversant with bush conditions and the psychology of the bush people. We had been able to compare notes, which had given us a clearer understanding than the newspapers could possibly have given their readers. Rowles had said one thing to one and something else to another, and yet a different version to a third, on one particular point. He had told so many lies. In my own experience he had told three different stories of how he acquired Ryan's truck.

We knew that men could disappear in the bush and their skeletons not be found for years afterwards, if ever. We knew that sometimes a member of the great floating population of Central Australia might have sound reasons for a voluntary disappearance. We knew that it would be possible – nay, probable – for Carron, Ryan, or Lloyd, to disappear voluntarily for some reason or other; but improbable, if not impossible, that three men about the same time should voluntarily disappear, and two of them give their property to "Snowy" Rowles.

For me, as for those others, it was impossible to disassociate the disappearance of Carron from that of Ryan and Lloyd. There came the rumour that Carron had been seen at work on a station after May, 1930; but I could not give this story credence. There was no rumour that Ryan or Lloyd had been seen after they went to Challi Bore, on Narndee Station, with Rowles.

Whilst the acorns dropped about me, whilst semi-consciously I wondered why someone did not gather them in to feed to a pig, I tried to imagine what Rowles's defence would be. What defence could he possibly put forward? How was he going to explain his possession of those two watches? How account for the shirts of a kind not sold in Australia? How explain the strange fact that the rifle Carron look away from Wydgee Station was found in his hut on Hill View Station? How was he going to account for two full days, May 18 and 19, 1930, which he said he had spent at Windimurra homestead, and which three witnesses had said, in effect, he had not?

If he left Carron trapping at the Windimurra homestead when he went to Paynesville to cash Carron's cheque, why did he go direct to Youanmi from Paynesville? Why in the name of common sense did he not reply to Lemon's telegram of inquiry when it was given to him and he knew it was a reply-paid telegram?

That Carron was dead, who could doubt after having seen the relics found in the ashes of a fire on a Government Reserve, relics that had been identified at the inquest by Carron's wife, by Carron's jeweller, and by Carron's dentist?

Candidly, it appeared incredible. It was so difficult to believe that the Snowy Rowles we knew was in the dock of a criminal court. It was equally difficult to believe that the Snowy Rowles we knew had, one day in March, 1926, snatched a bag containing

£300 from a shop girl in Perth; and that in 1928 he had robbed several country stores on the eastern wheat-belt.

An acorn fell with painful effect on the back of my hand which rested on the bench. Summer was nearly over.

And for you, Snowy, alas, the winter has come!

The Bones

After months of preparation, the Crown had at length declared its case against John Thomas Smith, known as "Snowy" Rowles. To the Court it introduced Constable Hearn, who detailed his finding of the fire at the 183 Government Reserve, and the items he discovered among the ashes. Detective-Sergeant Manning clearly described the course of his investigation, by which he had built up a wonderful case from the very sands of the Murchison.

Dr. William McGillivray, the Government Pathologist, now gave evidence regarding the human bones submitted to him for examination. One of the packages given him contained fragments of a human skull. Small bones in a tobacco-tin, he said, might be those of human fingers or toes, or animal paws or toes – he was doubtful which. The contents of a matchbox were burned human teeth, one of which was a molar tooth. Other teeth shown to him he declared to be artificial teeth. He would not say if the pieces of skull bones were those belonging to the skull of a white man or an aboriginal. He thought no one could tell that.

Dr. McKenzie, who sat on the witness stand with plaster casts of human skulls on the table before him, stated that he thought that pieces of bone when built into larger pieces indicated that they did belong to the skull of a white man.

The Book Plot

Arthur William Upfield deposed how he searched for a method of destroying a human body; how he found it; the details of it.

When Lancelot Bowen Maddison, the boundary-rider north of my former section was called, he was asked if he knew Rowles. He replied: "I know him well. I first met him on the fence just north of the Camel Station, soon after I commenced work there. He was then riding a motor-cycle in the course of his duties as an employee of Narndee Station. I saw him frequently after that. I was at the Camel Station one night with Arthur Upfield, David Coleman, George Ritchie, and Rowles. We all joined in a discussion of Upfield's projected book, The Sands of Windee. We particularly referred to the disposal of a murdered man's remains."

Carron's Dentist

Arthur William Sims, dentist, of Hamilton, N.Z., said he had attended a patient named Leslie George Brown, and he identified the photographs of Louis John Carron as Brown. On August 1, 1929, he made a complete lower denture for Brown, and also filled several upper teeth. On August 20 he placed a small amalgam filling in the biting surface of one of Brown's upper molars.

Mr. Gibson, Crown Prosecutor, handing witness teeth found in the fire ashes near the bore at the 183-mile, asked:

"Do you find there four upper inciser pin teeth and a number of diatoric teeth, making a complete lower denture save for one incisor?"

Witness: "That is so."

After carefully examining the molar tooth found in one of the ash heaps near the bore, witness said:

"It has a drill hole in it in exactly the same place as the hole I drilled in Brown's molar tooth. The filling has gone from this tooth. The amalgam filling I placed in Brown's tooth would not stand up to great heat."

Carron's Jeweller

Thomas Andrew Long said that he was up to March, 1927, a jeweller trading in Queen Street, Auckland, N.Z. After examining the gold ring found with other relics in the camp fire-site, witness said it appeared to be one of his own faceted wedding rings. It was marked "18 ct., Red. 1286, M.C." He had a letter in his possession from the wholesale jewellers saying that rings marked in that fashion were made only in New Zealand.

Mr. Curran, defending Rowles: "I suppose that in the course of a year a good many wedding rings marked like that one would be sold throughout New Zealand?"

Witness: "Yes, that would be so."

Mr. Curran: "How can you be so sure that you cut and rejoined that particular ring for Mrs. Brown (Carron's wife)?"

Witness: "At the time Mrs. Brown wanted the ring altered I was very busy and my chief assistant was away. I gave the ring to an assistant who was not an expert goldsmith. He botched the job, and had I not been so busy I would have dropped the ring into the melting pot and cut another. This ring is of 18 carat gold, and my assistant re-joined the cut ends with a 9 carat gold solder. The lighter shade of the solder against the ring itself has not been destroyed by the fire."

The ring was handed to the jurymen, each of whom examined it intently. After the trial it came out that the ring with its 9 carat gold solder was the deciding factor in their verdict.

In his statement made to Detective-Sergeant Manning, the accused said that he picked up Carron at an outcamp named Condon on Wydgee Station, and that he brought him on to The Fountain outcamp where John Lemon then was camped in the employ of Narndee Station. The next day they went on to Watson's Well, on the Vermin Fence, then northward along the Fence to the 206-mile gate where the road between Youanmi and Mount Magnet passes through the fence. From there they went on and camped at the old deserted homestead of Windimurra Station.

The statement continues: "The next day I went to Paynesville, about 15 miles away, in my truck. Carron agreed to cut in the money for the goods we wanted, and gave me the Wydgee cheque for £25/0/7 to cash for him. I waited until sundown for the licensee to return from a mine he was working. I stayed the night at the hotel. The next day I returned to our camp, and gave Carron 4/8/- and the publican's own cheque for 16. The following night we went to Mount Magnet together, arriving between nine and ten o'clock. We had supper together at Joe Slavin's shop. Carron, who was a teetotaller, objected to my having a few drinks that night, and said he could do better alone. He took his gear off the truck. I went back to the hotel, and Carron came after me and reckoned he might be unable to cash Moses's cheque (the Paynesville publican) as it was made out in my name. So I gave him 16 for it. When I cashed Carron's cheque I endorsed Carron's name on the back. After giving Carron the cash I walked back into Mr. Rodan's bar. When the hotel closed at eleven o'clock I returned to the truck and drove five or six miles along the Youanmi road, where I went to sleep till morning, when I continued the journey to Jones' hotel at Youanmi. I only heard that Carron was missing last Monday when I saw something in a Murchison paper. Carron went on to Geraldton. He wrote me from there -"

Rebuttals

The manager, the overseer, and various stockmen swore that Rowles and Carron never camped at the old deserted homestead through which they passed. Just before leaving the Paynesville Hotel the accused told the licensee that he was going to Wiluna on a prospecting trip.

It was definitely proved that instead of returning to the old Windimurra homestead, and Carron, Rowles went direct to Youanmi, a distance of about 70 miles. He left Paynesville at about ten o'clock, and he arrived at Youanmi at 12:30 the same morning.

That was on May 21. The records of the Youanmi Post Office, and the evidence of the Post Master, showed that that afternoon Rowles took the Post Master to a station homestead in his truck to deliver a telegram.

When on the witness stand Rowles, being confronted with this, amended his statement, and said that he had forgotten that trip to Youanmi. He still maintained, however, that he returned to Carron after leaving Paynesville. He was neatly trapped into saying that he was not in Youanmi on May 22, and at a carefully calculated moment the astute Crown Prosecutor produced evidence to prove his lie. He produced the Youanmi storekeeper's docket book containing the carbon copies of the sales he had made on May 21 and 22. The first entry for May 22 was "S. Rowles, pair overalls, 11/6."

The Summing-Up

Mr. Justice Draper in his summing up said:

"Some of the statements made by Rowles in this case were hard to reconcile with those to be expected from a man who had committed no crime. It is for you, gentlemen of the jury, to decide. You are the ones to decide, but perhaps you will find it difficult to reconcile the statements made by Rowles as to his movements with Carron, with the evidence given in this court. The Crown case was that Carron had been murdered and the bones broken up into very small pieces, and distributed in heaps of ashes.

"There is a curious thing in this case, and I mention it for what it is worth. Upfield gave evidence that he was in the neighbourhood for some time. He says he remembers a discussion one night in a small room when the accused was among others present on October 6th, 1929. I suppose they want something to do in the bush," observed his Honor dryly. "Anyway, the interesting subject of discussion was how a human body could be destroyed without leaving any trace. The indications are that the method then dismissed was carried out in this case, but whether Rowles did it is a matter for you to decide."

Discussing the question of whether the skull bones were from the head of a European or aborigine, his Honor said they might ask themselves, remembering the articles found in the ashes with them, was it usual for natives to wear shoes with eyelets, was it usual for them to wear artificial teeth in the upper and lower jaws, and did they wear gold wedding rings.

"It would be a strange coincidence," observed his Honor, "seeing that Carron possessed things identical to all these articles, if those found in the fire did not belong to him."

The Verdict

The jury retired at five minutes to four on Saturday afternoon, and returned to give their verdict at six o'clock that same day. Rowles was brought up. Whilst waiting for Mr. Justice Draper to take his seat, whilst standing on the steps of the dock, he craned his head to see if he could read his fate on the faces of the jurymen. Failing that he turned to look at the massed witnesses. When the judge did take his seat, the accused mounted quickly into the dock, to stare hard at the jury. He was seen to shake his head, as if he knew that he was doomed.

"Guilty."

The dread word sounded like two strokes of a bell in the hushed court.

Asked if he had anything to say, Rowles replied in a steady voice:

"I have been found guilty of a crime that has never been committed."

"Is that all? Is that all you have to say?" asked the judge.

Rowles remained silent.

The hush was broken by the judge's voice pronouncing the sentence of death.

Appeal Fails

Rowles through his counsel, Mr. Fred Curran, appealed to the Supreme Court of Western Australia on the grounds that:—

(a) Evidence relating to the disappearance of two men named James Ryan and George Lloyd and to my association with them was wrongfully admitted. (At the hearing it came out that it was Rowles's own counsel who first brought in the matter of Ryan and Lloyd.)

(b) That the trial judge wrongfully admitted evidence by one, Arthur William Upfield, a novelist, to the effect that during October, 1929, I was present and took part in a discussion relating to the disappearance of human bodies. And that I had been arrested on another charge and had escaped from legal custody.

(c) That there was no evidence that Louis Carron was dead.

(d) That the learned trial judge misdirected the jury on the evidence.

(e) The trial resulted in a miscarriage of justice.

The State Full Court unanimously dismissed the appeal.

Counsel for Rowles then appealed to the High Court, of Australia, sitting in Melbourne, and this court rejected the application tor the appeal to he heard by it, by a two to one majority.

A public petition was organized by the Groper Brotherhood and Housewives Association, and finally presented to the Attorney General. A public meeting was held at a theatre to urge Rowles's reprieve. Letters appeared in the papers appealing for clemency for the sake or his mother.

The Curtain Falls

But Rowles was hanged on the morning of June 13, without making a confession; although the relatives of George Lloyd wrote urging the condemned man to say something regarding the fate of Lloyd.

Some few days before the end Snowy Rowles made a dramatic statement from the condemned cell. He said that on his return from Paynesville to his camp he found that Carron had accidentally poisoned himself with poisoned butter baits used for foxes. That, as he was an escaped prisoner, he feared to inform the police and he burned the body.

It. had no effect but to confirm his guilt, for he could not possibly have gone back to Windimurra, found his mate, taken the body fifty odd miles and burned it, then travelled to Youanmi, another 67 miles in two hours and a quarter.

Thus passed out a strangely stormy spirit. His life before him, favoured by the gods with a fine physique and good looks, he could have risen high in this country, impelled upward by the personality of his Doctor Jekyll; but the secret devil in all of us, the Mr. Hyde, was too powerful for "Snowy" Rowles.

Ryan's ute, with Rowles' gun.

Police exhibits for the Snowy Rowles case.

Novels by Arthur W. Upfield:

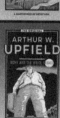

Printed in Australia
Ingram Content Group Australia Pty Ltd
AUHW010843060224
390046AU00005B/14

9 781922 473721